AF445765

SIMPLE CROCHET FOR
BEGINNERS

Learn to Crochet in Easy and Simple Innovating Patterns (volume 1).

PETER WHITY

TABLE OF CONTENTS

INTRODUCTION

This book is useful for all crocheters, even those with no past knowledge or experience and those with more specialized skills. If you have never made used of a crochet hook or any of the tools before but want to practice, this book series will guide you through all of the simple stitches so you can create wonderful small and big pieces. Unless you already understand how to crochet, you'll love this project.

This book series will guide you through a step-by-step technique to any form of crochet patterns and how you can become a professional in this field.

Once you become confident with all forms of crochet stitches as you go through the book series we will show you different projects that you can do by yourself.

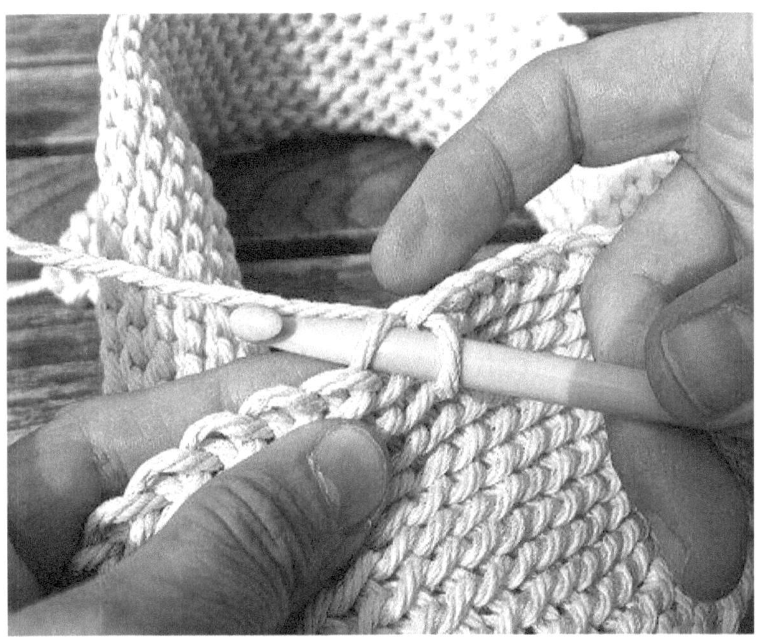

PART 1: UNDERSTANDING CROCHET

BRIEF HISTORY:

Crochet is a term used by the French, Belgians, Italians, including Spanish-speaking citizens. In Holland, the art is recognized as haken, in Denmark as haekling, in Norway as heckling, as well as in Sweden as virkning.

CROCHET LACE VS CHAIN LACE

Annie Potter, a crochet specialist as well as a world traveler from the United States, claims that "Real crochet as we understand it today was created during the sixteenth part of the century". In France, it was recognized as 'crochet lace,' and in England, it was classified as 'chain lace.'" Walter Edmund Roth met ancestors of the Guiana Indians in 1916, she says, and found traces of authentic crochet.

However, according to Paludan, the simple truth is that "There is no conclusive proof as to how old or where the craft of crochet originated". Crochet was almost unknown in Europe until the year 1800. Some reports suggest that crochet dates back to the 1500s in Italy, were it was known as 'nun's work' or 'nun's lace,' and was used by nuns for church textile materials "she describes.

Her studies turned up several samples of lace-making as well as a type of lace tape, both of which have been retained, but "all signs are that crochet was not established in Italy as early as the 16th century"—under either name.

WHAT IS CROCHET?

Crochet is a textile-making technique that involves interlocking loops of wool, fabric, or other materials with a crochet needle. Crochet was firstly noticed in France from the French word "crochet", which means small hooks. Steel, wood, bamboo, and plastic are some of the materials that can be used to make hooks.

PART 2: BENEFITS OF CROCHETING

If crocheting is taking up the most amount of your time. Sometimes, you will feel compelled to explain your hobby and feel doubtful mostly if you are not getting it right. There are far more than enough practice exercises in the upcoming series that will show you why crocheting is a perfect way to spend your free time, but here are a few of the most compelling.

The followings are the benefits you will derive from crochet:

STRESS BUSTER:

Nothing boosts focusing on a design you like, along with the continuous utilization of your hands as well as the fun feel of the yarn, to keep your mind off your worries.

REDUCE DEPRESSIONS:

Crochet has been shown to assist with more severe problems like depression, in addition to general tension and worry.

HAND EXERCISE:

Crocheting has established beneficial effects, as the small repeated motions involved will keep your wrists, limbs, and fingers supple in consistent movement.

ACTIVE MIND:

All of these things allow you to keep the thought of patterns sharp; something many experts say will help avoid disorders like Alzheimer's.

LEAD TO CREATIVITY:

Creating something that brings joy to you or others provides a great deal of fulfillment.

Other benefits are:

- Lead to comfort and relaxation of the mind.

- It helps to increase self-esteem.

- Happiness and joy mostly when you finally accomplished a project.

- Breaking of bad habits.

PART 3: TYPES OF CROCHET

Below are the types of crochet we have:

TAPESTRY CROCHET:

This is the crochet that is comparable of color-work; it's also referred to as intarsia crochet. There are several diverse techniques of working in tapestry crochet as well as each design gives a diverse outcome. Tapestry crochet among the numerous ways to do color-work.

SYMBOL CROCHET:

This stitch is also recognized as a graph or chart crochet, which is used in many Japanese stitch books. It's a very handy ability to have so you can use those symbol crochet books in any language to create the projects simply by following the map.

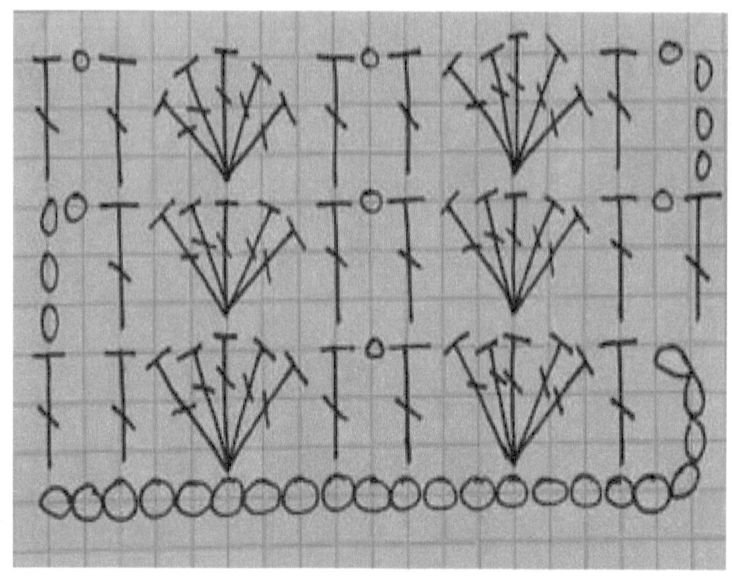

STAINED GLASS CROCHET:

Almost equivalent to overlay crochet, except the top part is usually done in black yarn to produce a stained glass effect. Crochet in a unique as well as eye-catching style.

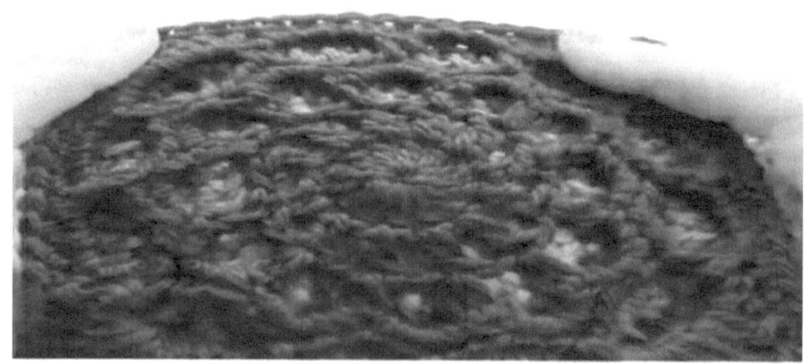

AMIGURUMI CROCHET:

This is a Japanese form of crochet art style that applies to the creation of tiny plush toys or critters out of knitted as well as crocheted yarn. Nuigurumi implies a stuffed doll while ami implies crochet or draw. It's amigurumi when you see a small doll or toy crafted out of wool. Common amigurumi themes include Hello Kitty, Plants vs. Zombies, including Mario Kart. Thins you can make are toys and fan items etc.

RIBBED CROCHET:

Ribbed is also known as cabled crochet. It's a chunky crochet pattern of interconnecting cables that can be found to create beanies, sweaters, including scarves.

Aran is indeed a yarn weight, so keep that in mind anytime you see the term "Iran" in a design. When you see a snapshot of someone snuggled up under a large, warm blanket, it makes you feel good.

Things you can create with ribbed crochet are:

coats	jackets
blankets	lapgans
Body cover	scarves

BAVARIAN CROCHET:

This is an antique crochet stitch that is usually used to make granny squares in circles. It provides a dense fabric with a finer texture than granny squares and makes for more gradual color changes. Each column is divided into two sections: a base row of clusters as well as a top line of shells. Bavarian crochet resembles a rather fancy version of granny squares.

You can create blankets and shawls with Bavarian crochet.

BOSNIAN CROCHET:

Bosnian crochet uses only the crochet slipping stitch, which is performed in separate sections of a stitch from the prior row to produce a dense, knit-like cloth. Bosnian crochet hooks are available in stores, but standard crochet hooks can also be used. Shepherd's knitting is another name for it. It also resembles knitting in appearance. It's not a very fashionable look right now, as well as if you see it, you'll probably assume it's knitted.

BULLION CROCHET:

This is a highly advanced crochet stitch that is made by wrapping several yarn wraps over a very lengthy hook to create a distinctive as well as unusual 'roll' stitch. Bullion crochet is typically used during motifs rather than projects that include yarn. It produces a piece with a dense, standardized circular motif.

PINEAPPLE CROCHET:

This seems more like a common stitch as well as shape style rather than it being a technique. Pineapples can be used to make doilies as well as scarves, and sometimes even clothes in crochet. If you've figured out how to find a crochet pineapple, you'll see them all over the place. This stitching style gained prominence in the 1970s.

OVERLAY CROCHET:

A procedure in which stitches are applied to a base of crochet to make a created pattern. This brings up a lot of opportunities for color-work that is both elegant and complex.

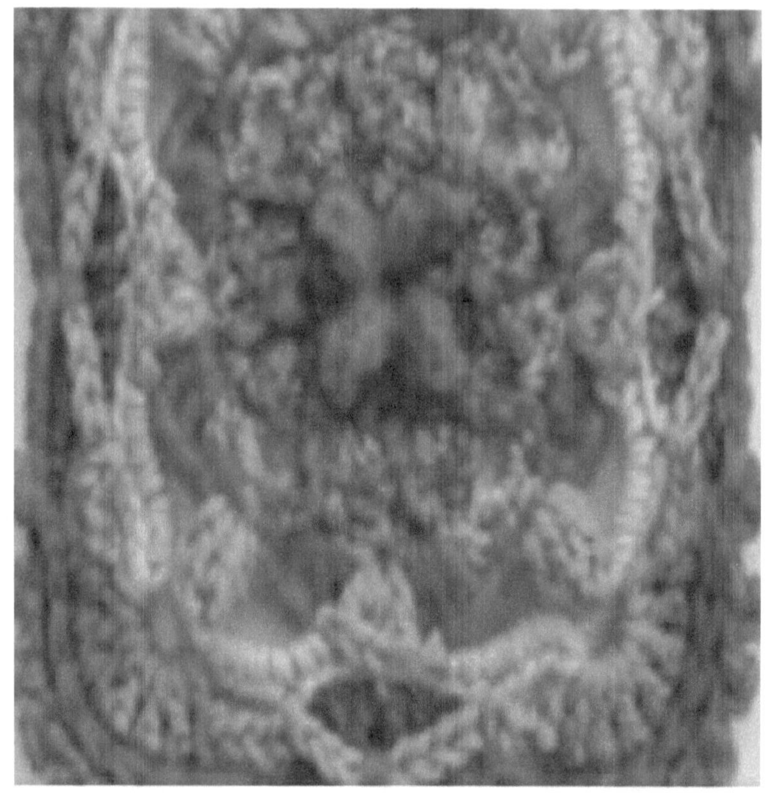

MICRO CROCHET:

This is a traditional crochet design that uses very fine yarn as well as fine crochet hooks. This is a delicate project that is perhaps better suited to more patient crocheters. You can use micro crochet to make the talisman, teen tiny and embellishments, etc.

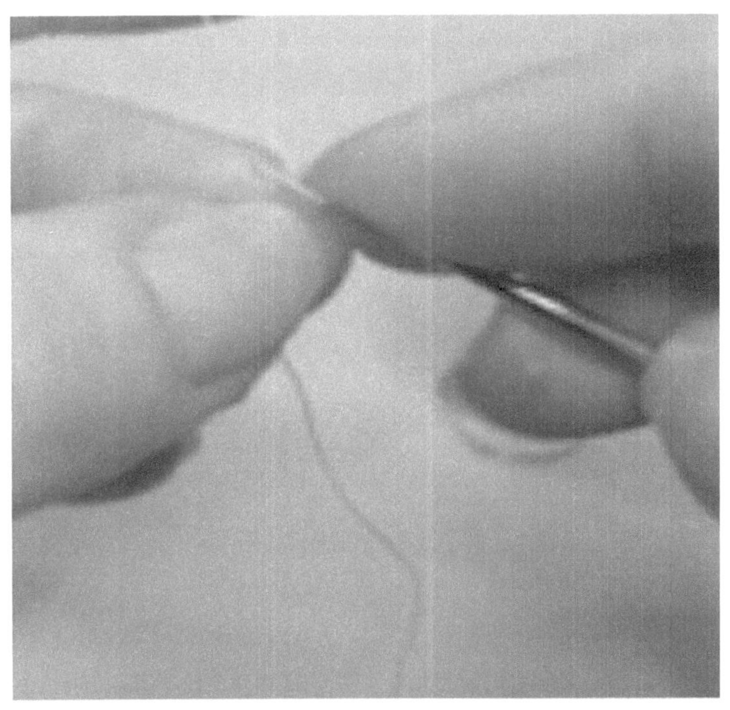

HAIRPIN CROCHET:

This is closely related to broomstick crochet, besides the crochet part is kept elastic among two thin metal rods and handled using a conventional crochet hook. This technique was named after the metal hairpins that were used when it was made. This technique produces a truly one-of-a-kind finished fabric.

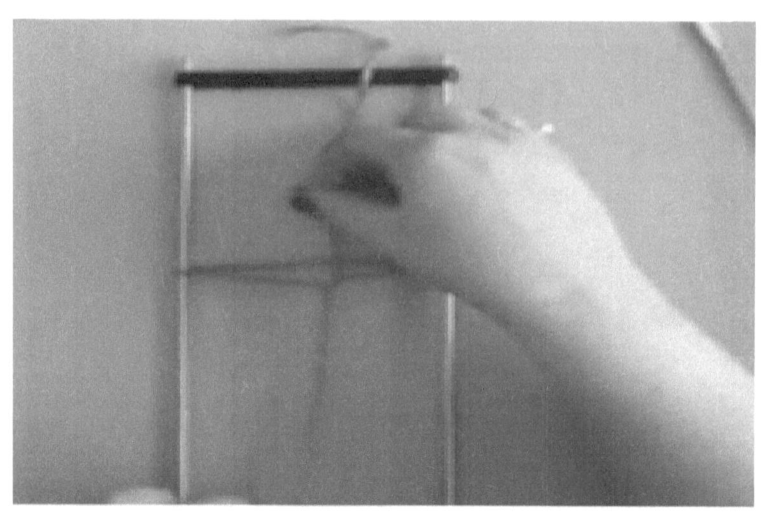

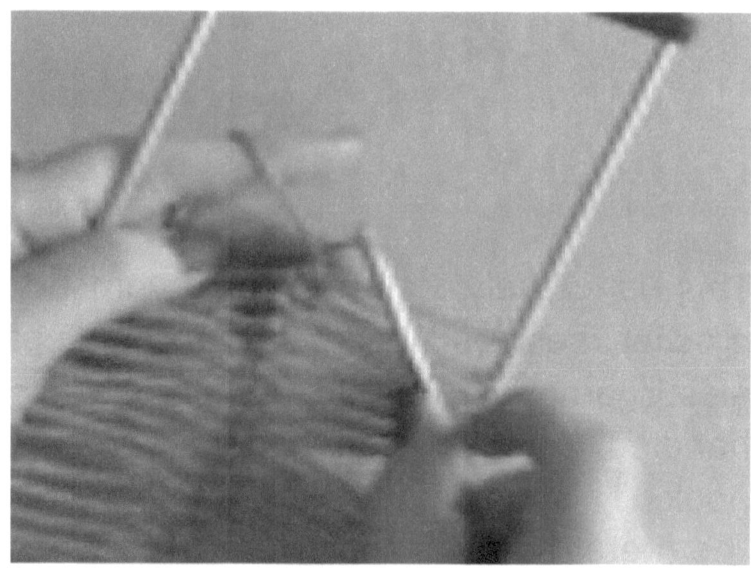

FREEFORM CROCHET:

This crochet style is made without the use of a pattern or an official plan. Crochet in this style is very organic and decorative. Note that if you're a disciplined person, this style might not be for you. If you're like me and fail without guidance or a strategy, stay away from freeform.

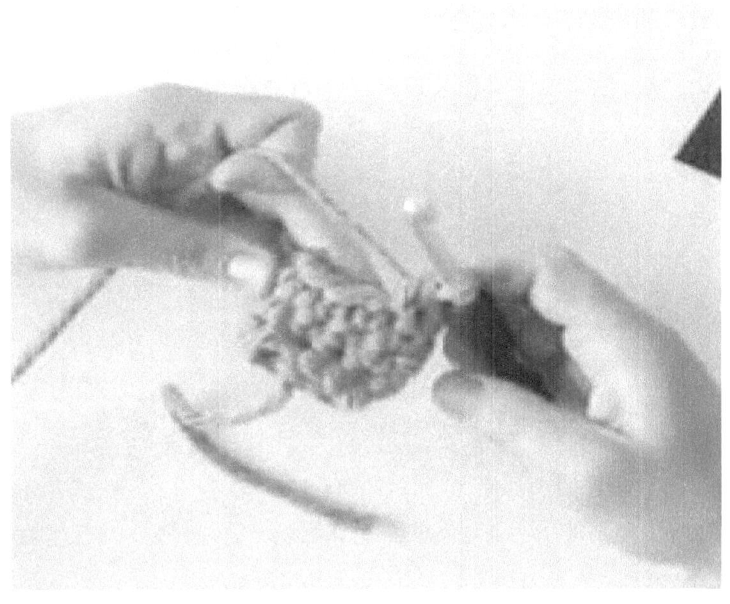

FINGER CROCHET:

Finger crochet is identical to finger knitting except that, it is crocheting without any of the needles. It's a kind of hand-woven fabric in the design of crochet stitching. Finger crochet is enjoyable when you first begin, but since the finishing tension is very loose, you'll want to switch to a hook and make more versatile projects sooner rather than later.

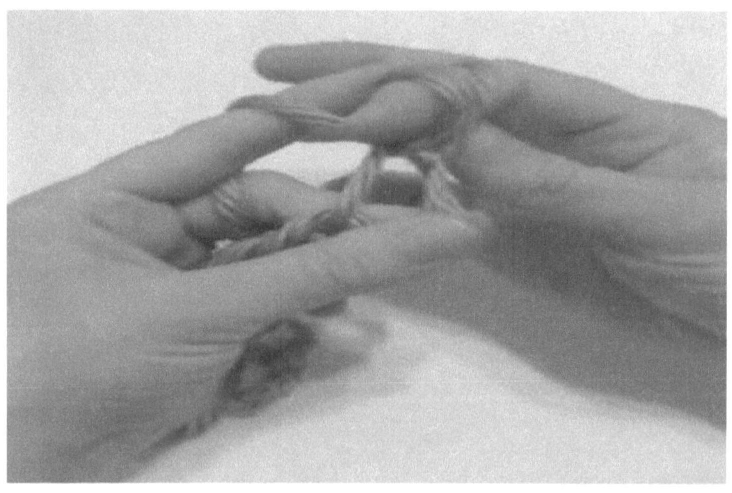

FILET CROCHET:

Chains as well as double crochet are used to produce this crochet design. It's a grid-like design of squares that are either filled enough or not filled and perhaps downbeat space which is used. it is used to create imagery design inside the object. The exquisiteness of filet crochet is that you can use both the entire and empty squares of the fabric to insert the design.

BROOMSTICK CROCHET:

This antique crochet stitch, also known as jiffy lace, is made with a conventional crochet hook except the stitches are built through something long as well as thick such as a broomstick handle. This day, most crocheters use wide crochet hooks or a heavy dowel to make broomstick lace. Broomsticks are nice and it is a perfect crochet technique to master because it creates a gorgeous and one of a kind finished product.

BRUGES CROCHET:

This technique is used to produce Bruges lace, which consists of creating crochet "ribbons" that are then crocheted with each other to form elaborate lace designs. Many grandmothers have several Bruges-style crochet pieces tucked away in drawers, covered in acid-free paper.

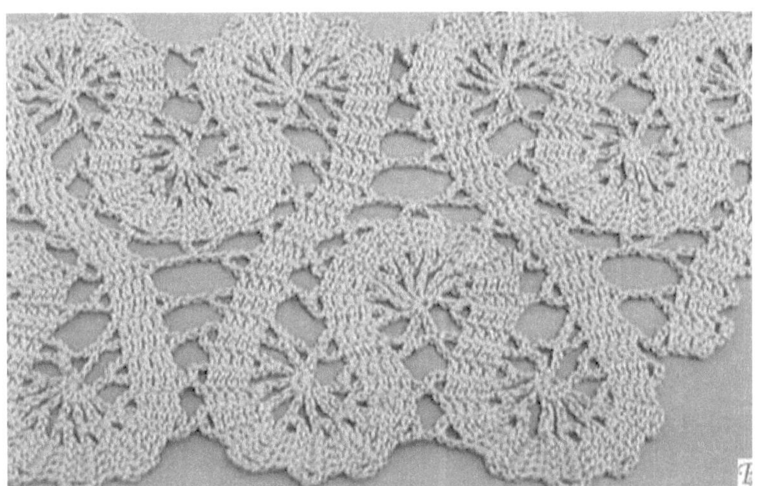

CLOTHESLINE CROCHET:

Modern crochet stitches are worked over a thick rope or clothesline-style stretch of thick twine to create round mats as well as baskets that maintain their form. This is a trial method that can be traced back to Nepalese and African craftspeople. You can use it to make mats and baskets.

CLONES LACE CROCHETS:

This crochet style is closely related to Irish lace crochet and then was developed as a faster and simpler alternative to needlepoint lace. The Clones method of knot is a crochet skill that comes with the Clones crochet skill collection. Clones lace is a very realistic crochet pattern that was used in wartime for utilitarian reasons.

CRO-HOOK CROCHET:

This form of crocheting uses a double-ended form of the hook to make double-sided crocheted items. It enables the crocheter to stitched on or off, at any end of their crochet piece, with no correct or incorrect hand. Cro-knit is another name for this. This design is close to traditional Tunisian crochet and creates outstanding colorwork that is difficult to achieve in other crochet types.

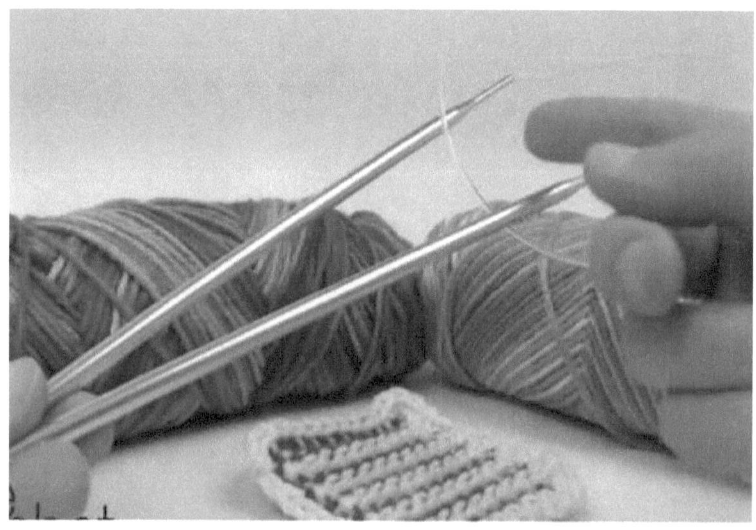